Saving Money

Also by Joe Atikian

CUBA UNDER EMBARGO:
The Macro Impact

INDUSTRIAL SHIFT:
The Structure of the New World Economy

Saving Money
The Missing Link

2nd Edition

Love Saving,
Grow Your Wealth

Joe Atikian

SAVING MONEY
2nd Edition
Copyright © Joe Atikian, 2014
First published in 2011

Cover design by Joe Atikian

If you enjoy this book, please consider writing a review on Amazon.com or your bookseller's website.

Please follow me on Twitter @joe_atikian
For more info see www.savingmoneybook.com
or www.atikian.com

Table of Contents

1 – First Things First

"I've been rich and I've been poor.
Rich is better."

(disputed origin; Sophie Tucker, Beatrice Kaufman, and several others)

Never mind being rich, whatever you think that rich means. The more realistic goal is to become better off than you are right now, and the only way to get there is by saving money. In your financial world, *better off* means having more in the bank so that you have the freedom to do some of the things that are always on your mind. You don't like the bank? That's ok, we'll talk more about that soon. Meanwhile, let's focus on making some improvement without the usual silliness about drinking less coffee or brown-bagging your lunch.

How can you enjoy daily life if you don't have any money? I'm not talking about having an income. Income is usually the money that you earn and spend every week. If you spend it, it simply ain't yours any more. Instead, I'm talking about having a pile of money just sitting there. Sure, having a solid income is good, but it's not enough to keep your worries away.

An income is not enough to keep you safe. As soon as you spend your income, you are back to nothing. Nor is an income enough to get your boss off your back or to buy a house or a car. So build a pile of money, and you can live better. It doesn't even matter very much how big the pile is. Having a pile of money will let you focus on some of the things that are most important to you. Then you can actually choose what you want to do – that's real power.

-    -   -   -   -

With so many books, websites, and blogs about the tedious business of saving money, there is no need to repeat the hundreds of details and tactics that you have already heard about. But there is a need to clearly show why those tactics don't work very well. It's because they are all based on fear, discipline, sacrifice, and math (maybe all the things that you dislike).

Instead, let's focus on the one truly indispensable point in the entire field of personal finance: feeding the incentive to save. Without saving, little else matters. You will have no choices, and it's hard to make anything happen. But now you'll see how saving money can be made easy and highly enjoyable instead of tedious.

Before getting started, we need to quickly distinguish a tactic like coupon clipping from saving money. They are not the same thing. For example, coupons may help to stretch your spending but they will not help you save your money. Just think, have you ever found a coupon, say for a $2 'saving' and then put $2 into a jar or in the bank in order to actually save it? No.

Try a much larger example. Have you found a sale on last year's car model? Perfect, go ahead and buy it. Choosing a lower priced item is rational, and clearly the better option compared to a high-priced item. But if you don't put that discount money in the bank and leave it alone, then this bargain will not result in saving money. So while there is nothing wrong with stretching your spending, and in fact it helps you to live better, it simply has very little to do with saving.

Fact # 1 : Saving Money means to *put it aside* and not touch it.

Bargain hunting and coupon clipping also distract you from saving money, because saving ends up as a side-effect. You might say that, "If I find a discount then I will save some money". In other words, you believe that saving is the result of some other action instead of something that you deliberately set out to do. But, more importantly, the focus on bargain hunting means that saving becomes a lower priority than spending. That is the common trap that prevents people from growing their wealth and improving their financial life.

We have barely started, and yet we've already found two traps that savers often fall into. Discipline and bargain hunting. Here is why people fall into the discipline trap or the bargain trap. It sounds easy until you actually try it. But how long do you think you could stand to push yourself to save pennies if that is not what you normally do? Could you be convinced to scrimp and remain steadfastly disciplined for years? I guess not. You either need to find a new way to achieve your saving goal, or you will likely just give it up. Soon we'll see how you can make these traps easy to avoid.

2 - Why It Usually Goes Wrong

Save your money. You heard it from your parents. You heard it on TV. You may have heard it from a financial advisor. You may have heard it from the wealthy barber. And the reason everyone tells you to save up is clear and practical. You should do it because it's good for you.

You always do what's good for you. You only have one drink a day. You don't smoke. You obey the speed limit and drink lots of water. All because it's good for you. Most importantly, you don't procrastinate. That's the big one because it involves doing the things that you hate doing. Who wants to cut the grass or organize their desk? It's a drag but you sacrifice the time and do it.

Of course nobody does what is good for them every time. That's mostly because there are no immediate consequences. It's easy to put off doing chores and being disciplined if the results don't appear until later.

Saving money, you are told, is in the same category as cutting the grass. You know you should do it. But it's also a drag. So you procrastinate, putting it off until you feel like doing it which, of course, is never. It doesn't help that saving is intensely discouraged because of the way it's presented, as a chore or a duty, like flossing your teeth. You might eventually get around to it but it's no joy. Or is it?

It's easy to see that the joy in cutting grass is not in the doing, but in the result. You actually enjoy looking at it, and you might have one or two beers on the deck after it's done. Organizing your desk goes the same way, and is even better. You may enjoy its appearance after it's done and it makes your work day easier. There is less annoyance each time you need to find something. Eventually though, the grass and your desk revert to their original mess, and you have to start all over again.

The reality is that saving your money is very different from doing chores. Saving is fun. You should be psyched about it but you first need to change your mind about what saving money does for you. And not only will you enjoy it, but unlike the grass that grows back or the desk that gets messy again, saving is permanent and the enjoyment keeps growing. It's easy to start, easy to keep it going, good for you, and fun. Hard to believe, and yet it's true. Read on and see how it works.

3 - Three Easy Pieces

How can saving money possibly be easy and enjoyable when everyone says it takes years of discipline? First, change your mind. Next, open a separate account for saving. Last, keep adding to it (even if it's in small bits). Is that all there is? Well, that's basically it, although the first part is the hardest because we are continuously trained to dislike saving. Psyche. Changing your mind may take a couple of steps, but you probably know what those steps are. No, not avoiding take-out coffee. Instead you just need to undo the negative psyche and then get to it.

As much as your parents tell you to save, they never tell you why you will like it. You hear about the unavoidable pain of saving but never about the joy. You hear about making sacrifices to save, but not about the new choices that saving brings. You hear about the discipline required, but never about the relief from daily stress. Pain, sacrifice, and discipline. Groan.

Even professional advocates of saving money turn you off. The banker in the TV ad says that the big banks are going to pinch you with excessive fees, but you can save a bit of money if you switch to his bank. The head of the central bank says that saving money will prevent national economic trouble. Financial planners say you will retire in poverty if you don't save. Getting pinched? Economic trouble? Poverty? So much negativity naturally leads to a big turn off and it's easy to see the effects. National savings levels are low, and personal debt is high. Somehow, all of those professional people who try to encourage saving are confused about why it turned out this way.

The only thing that drives people is desire. So it's completely natural that we just ignore all the sour messages and instead focus on our immediate wants. That would be shopping, dining, or travel. Everyone wants love, security, a full belly, and a full closet. A beautiful house or a major renovation would be nice too, along with a new car. Oh, and some new shoes. Saving money and new shoes don't go together (at least according to scrimpers, budgeters and coupon clippers) so people will just ignore the saving for a while.

So if all the experts actually turn off our drive to save, couldn't we simply encourage each other to do it? After all, people discuss real estate, cars, and clothes all the time. It's almost a social pastime in which they brag, compare notes or complain. Don't they discuss their wages or salary in the same way? Sometimes they do, such as in unionized workplaces where all of the wages in a collective agreement are regularly published. But, in reality, talking about real estate is just a substitute for talking about salary because someone can get a pretty good idea of your household income from what you say about housing prices. So it turns out that people will strongly hint at their income even if they don't discuss it openly. When it comes to saving though, things get strangely quiet.

For some reason saving money is the most private of all possible topics. Can you just imagine this in a casual chat: "Hey, Jim, how much do you have in the bank?" This practically never happens. Saved up money is totally invisible, and that makes saving as desirable as getting a dental filling. You usually avoid it. You feel better once you have it, but nobody else can tell whether you got one or not. Likewise, the total silence about saving money doesn't bring any appeal to doing it. You may show people around your lovely home, but you will never chat about your great success at saving money. In the end, financial professionals haven't convinced us to save money, and we haven't convinced ourselves.

-        -   -   -   -

There is a list of good reasons to save. Save for a rainy day. Not bad, but it's not too inspiring is it?

Save for something big. That means you should save in order to spend big and end up exactly where you started, with no spare money. Not too clever is it?

Save for retirement. That one works too, but it tells you to spend like a miser during your younger life so that you can spend like a miser through your older life. Not so motivating is it?

All of these worn out reasons have one feature in common: they portray your financial affairs as dreary. The promise of being stuck in a world of low-spending boredom will never move anyone to change their ways.

Many factors push people away from saving money, while the taboo around discussing it doesn't help pull people toward it. And most strangely, all the players from parents to bankers to financial advisers keep on missing the obvious path to saving money: the desire to do it. Almost everyone says that they want to save more money, but throughout our lives the authorities have concentrated on the negative and the difficult view of saving. They have also ignored the reasons to desire it. More precisely, they have beaten the desire to save out of us. Once you change your mind about it though, saving money changes your life in some important ways that you may not have expected.

Is there really a better approach than to treat saving as a private nuisance? Of course there is. Just direct your mental focus away from saving money as a task. Do it now. Stop thinking of it as a chore. Because, in fact, saving money isn't a chore.

Certainly not a big one. It doesn't require you to do anything more than put some money into the bank each time you get paid. The wealthy barber and the automatic millionaire have already explained this step clearly enough (even though they missed the most important link). If you think that's too much to do then you are finished before you start, so don't be that way. Stop it. Instead of dwelling on saving as a task, just take a minute to ponder the lovely money you have just saved. Then move on with your day.

So where is the fun? It's right here in 3 ways. At first, there's a bit of fun in watching this small stash of money grow. This feels really good. You'll soon realize that it's better to see $50 grow to $1,000 than it is to constantly struggle with a measly $40 balance at the ATM. This growing stash of cash is what you have always desired. For a while, you may even forget to pay any attention. Then suddenly, your balance is a lot bigger than you thought possible. It might be around $12,000. This leads to the second bit of fun: now you realize that you are growing financially stronger. You wanted this so very much, and now here it is. Desire fulfilled. This is good.

Now you have more flexibility to do things that were out of your reach just last year. More importantly, you have gained control and that too feels really good. You know that you can spend a bit, but you also know that you don't want to go back to your old position of financial weakness. Spending is now less appealing than saving exactly because you realize that spending leads to less power and less choices. Of course this is merely short term stuff. The real fun, the third part, is yet to come. Once your mindset is changed, your personal power grows. This is not just financial power any more. This is the big payoff to saving money.

4 - The Fun of Saving Money

Let's say you have succeeded in changing your view of saving money from a chore to an easy joy. You have opened a new savings account. You have arranged automatic deposits for about 10% of your pay check. If your weekly take home pay is $500 then $50 goes to savings, right away. Your account balance has grown to about $2,500 after the first year. That's the short term, and it's the period in which you have learned that living on $450 a week is pretty much the same as living on $500. Even if you never get a pay raise, your savings after 10 years will be about $30,000, assuming you can get interest at 3%.

If $30,000 doesn't sound life changing, think of the alternative. What would your position be if you hadn't saved? Your weekly $50 could have bought you some take out coffee, some magazines, or a movie and popcorn (these are all fine if that's what you want), but more importantly you would have zero in the bank and zero power to make choices in your job or in other parts of your life. You would have had more take out coffee but zero financial power.

Here is the falsehood that people keep accepting as true: the freedom to buy a few coffees is more fun than saving. And here is the truth about saving: financial power is way more fun than a few coffees. Just don't get the idea that the route to financial power involves fighting your desire for coffee, because it absolutely doesn't. You cannot fight your desires and you should not try because it doesn't work. More on that a bit later.

Look out a bit further in time, say 20 or 30 years. By the time most people are in their 40s or 50s, their habits are firmly set. With a $500 weekly pay check, that 30-year habit will get you over $150,000. That's with a modest 2% raise and 3% interest each year. If your weekly take home pay was $1,000 you would be sitting on more than $300,000. Now this is starting to look like a lot of fun, so start changing your mind about saving.

Take a small step back. If your take home pay was around $500 you are somewhere near the low end of wage earners. There is absolutely nothing wrong with this situation, but it leaves you with very little choice about your working life. You will likely need to accept whatever jobs are available and will have no realistic way out. If, instead, you had done 10 years of saving, your $30,000 balance would be life changing. Your thoughts have changed in the meantime and you may decide to take some job training in order to increase your earning power for the rest of your life.

Increased earnings, increased choices, and increased power sound like a lot more fun than the sour tones of "save your money". You could negotiate a pay raise or leave your job without having to pick up an extra room mate. You could start a small business on the side. Your choices are expanding, but you have also gotten rid of the daily nagging pressure that goes with having no money in the bank.

The big payoff is greater personal power. This means less mental grind and more freedom, which sounds a lot more like fun than a chore. And it is fun unless you spend it all on something unproductive and your finances revert to a mess just like a cluttered desk or an overgrown lawn.

5 - The Nuts and Bolts

This 10% saving level is not new, but it's not a hard rule either. You could just as well use 7% or 14%, so pick a number and do it. Using automatic deposits to make you forget about the 10% is another well-worn technique. These are very good steps and there are already a lot of books and other sources that recommend them. Go buy these books, or better yet, save your money and borrow them from a friend or library. They will explain the details very well. Even so, they haven't succeeded. You can see that people still don't like to save, because the dominant culture always portrays saving as a chore. The authors of these books still regret that they haven't had a more positive impact on people's saving habits. That's why they keep writing new books for you to buy.

This is the new part. Saving is most often portrayed as a chore where it should be seen as a joy. Saving shapes your frame of mind into enjoying your increasing wealth. In other words, saving is what you do in order to get wealth, which is something that you want. So when it comes to money, saving leads to joy. But in the meantime we are drowning in advertising that urges us to do the opposite, to spend.

Advertisers portray spending as a joy where it should be seen as risking your wealth and stability. Spending frames your mind to worry about your ATM balance, incoming bills, and debt repayment. So repeat: saving is not a chore. The only thing that needs to change is the way you think about saving. And in order to change your thinking, there are a few simple steps to take. Then get accustomed to enjoying financial growth.

Fact # 2 : Saving money is not a chore.

Most people would say that spending enables them to have material things or experiences: usually a house, a car, and other personal goods along with fine dining or vacations. They also say that saving takes away from these desirable things, the things that make up their so-called 'standard of living'. But what about the things that spending can't get you? Such as a temporary break to go back to school, or to make a job change. Or time to start a new business, or look after aging parents. What you don't hear people say is that saving provides flexibility, freedom, and power. Spending takes away from *these* desirable things.

So the nuts and bolts of saving has nothing to do with what percentage you should save or what kind of account you should open. It's really about how much value you place on the things you buy, the things that wear out (like cars) or the things that are gone as soon as you get back home (like vacations). Cars and vacations are perfectly good things, not to be avoided. But is an extra vacation so valuable that it should totally prevent the great experience of financial security, or the flexibility to leave your soul-sucking job?

Saving and spending are in nearly perfect balance. The more common view is one of truly perfect balance - that every dollar saved is a dollar that cannot be spent. That may seem right but it turns out to be a bit off the mark in two ways. It all depends on timing. If you do your saving first, then you can <u>earn</u> interest. But if you do the spending first, then you must <u>pay</u> interest (think about buying a car). So it turns out that the dollar you save is bigger than the dollar you spend.

Fact # 3 : The saved dollar is more powerful than the spent dollar.

      The second aspect of timing affects your power to make choices. If you save some money first, you have the freedom to decide how to spend some money later. You have the time to really think about your choice. But if you spend it all first, then you have eliminated the choice of saving and the financial power you could have had. So the nuts and bolts of saving is also about how to *arrange* your spending.

      Arrange your spending so that it happens *after* your saving. Repeat: if spending is the priority then it destroys your financial power.

Fact # 4 : Saving builds power; spending reduces power.

6 – Say No to Lifestyle Envy

One of the most powerful ideas about saving and spending has to do with the level of your lifestyle. What level do you think you are at? Do you compare yourself with others? Do you feel better off or worse off than your friends? This is all in your mind, but it can make or break you financially. One bad mental habit is to compare your material lifestyle to other people. It's a bad habit because you will always lose. Someone else always has more than you, so envy is truly pointless. Besides, envy is financially destructive. Envy pushes your spending higher which could cut into your savings and reduce your wealth. Don't ask whether or not you can afford something; instead ask whether you *want* to afford it. Once you build up your desire for financial power, you will be better able to see that spending is not the only way to enjoy your money.

How does this comparison thing work? Let's say that I have a slightly lower income than one of my neighbors. The flip side is that I have a higher income than another neighbor, so I shouldn't care. That's just an unavoidable reality anyway. Someone always has more than I do. But because incomes cannot be seen, the only thing that neighbors can compare is material possessions. So that's what neighbors do. And then they make the mistake of thinking that people with fewer possessions are financially weaker. Wrong.

Savers may have somewhat less stuff than non-savers, and they may have fewer restaurant meals, cars, or vacations. But along with that, savers will have more wealth. The idea is that saving a bit more leads you to having a bit less stuff than the neighbor, but the neighbor has less financial power than you. And of course you can enjoy your growing savings which, by the way, you could invest. And if you invest well, your wealth will grow even more. You can see the upward spiral already. Eventually the saver who ignores the neighbors is the one who can afford to choose, and may end up having more stuff than the non-saver. In the end it is mostly your attitude toward comparisons that determines your growing financial power. And financial power is a real part of your standard of living, just as real as possessions and experiences.

Look at some numbers. Does it matter a lot if you live like a $50,000 earner instead of a $45,000 earner? Of course not. It is nearly impossible to tell the difference. You are neither miserable nor living high relative to your coworkers in a similar income bracket. But the difference becomes hugely important if that $5,000 gap per year is put to pure saving for 30 years. The difference is over $300,000 in the bank. At 40 years it's over $500,000 in the bank. Half a million. What sounds like more fun? Being a 60 year old non-saver with zero, or a 60 year old saver with half a million in the bank? And remember, that wasn't 40 years of saving in penny-pinching misery and clipping coupons, it was 40 years of a barely noticeable difference in material lifestyle.

Does this mean that you must wait for 30 or 40 years for the fun of saving to kick in? No. It starts right away as you watch your new savings stash grow, and this is just the surface part of the ongoing fun. But the fun of saving isn't the same kind of fun as partying or socializing. It's more inside you, and way bigger. It's the ability to toy with your options at work, to be relaxed about paying for your home when mortgage rates or rents go up, or the freedom to change your life course mid-stream. Through that entire time you would have financial power, free choice, and less mental stress from being cash strapped.

Think for a minute about how this plays out daily. If you have no savings and if your bank balance is always under a couple hundred dollars, you are always stuck with no choices. You might have a roommate that you barely tolerate, and it is very difficult to make a change. In order to move to another place on your own you need to come up with 2 months of rent. Meantime the roommate might leave and you are short another month. There is nowhere nearly enough in the bank to cover this, so you are stuck. Maybe your employer treats you poorly, too. But you need every pay check badly, even before you get your hands on it. So you can't complain and you can't leave. Compare that major pain with the so-called pain of saving money.

If you had even a few thousand in the bank, things would be very different in your favor. The simplest pleasure in that case would be just looking at the nice bank balance. And it only gets nicer each week. It's already more fun than being stuck in last year's ditch. But it's also very reassuring to know that if your employer pushes you too far, you actually have the option of leaving. If your roommate becomes unbearable, you can get out on your own without getting into a financial mess. If a friend proposes starting a small web company, you can realistically consider joining in.

Just like watching your money grow is a pleasure, simply thinking about some new life changes is a pleasure. Consider this. Just having the option of making these changes makes your current situation more bearable. You don't actually have to make any changes, you just feel better knowing that you can do it if you want to. Of course doing any of these things would mean spending some of your savings, but this is strictly optional. You can choose to spend and rebuild if needed, whereas before the savings built up, there was no choice. So saving gives you choices, flexibility and peace of mind. You might even be less freaked out, more relaxed and productive at work, which might lead to … a raise?

Fact # 5 : Saved money gives you choices.

Although it's true that you can have a good time with $5,000 per year in extra spending, that is only one side of the story. And one-sided stories are deceptive. Doesn't the fun of spending the last $5,000 of your income merely hide the daily grind of having no spare money? Doesn't that spending prevent you from achieving something bigger like education, starting a business, or retiring early? If you have a big goal, keep it in mind when you decide to save. You don't have to think of it as nagging to reduce spending; that works against you. Rather your big goal is one of your desires that need feeding. Feed your big desires at least as much as your smaller ones.

Remember that your big goal is something that you want, not something that you are being forced to do. With that in mind, you can think about saving in a new way. So when a spending opportunity arises, remember your big goal and then decide on what you prefer. Do you prefer to spend for your immediate want or to save for your bigger wants? Will this bit of spending help or hurt the big goal? You can still decide, but now you will habitually consider both of your desires instead of always being biased toward the small one, or toward the short term. Shifting to a positive view of saving is strictly psychological. It has little to do with your income level.

Remember too, saving some money doesn't mean that you will not spend any more. You will still spend 90% of your income. You can still get take out coffee, vacations, or whatever. But you will trade just a few of these things for the new added joy of having financial power. Saving money is commonly viewed as a sacrifice, as a necessary evil that slightly lowers your standard of living. No such thing is true. Your standard of living has two parts: material and financial. *Every dollar you spend on material goods or experiences takes away from your financial power*. So saving decreases your spending, but it also increases your wealth.

Saving money increases your financial standard of living, which also improves your state of mind. Extra spending rarely improves your state of mind beyond the moment, but extra saving always does. Just think, who has a better standard of living? The person who spends an extra $5,000 or the one who saves it? The saver will end up with more money, more freedom, and a more relaxed frame of mind. And again, the saver who invests carefully usually ends up with more material possessions than the non-saver.

-    -   -   -   -

What about higher income earners. The word on the street is that there are as many high earners with no savings as there are in other income groups. But all of the same ideas apply here. If you take home $250,000 a year, are you fabulously ahead of someone with $225,000? No you aren't. Nobody can really tell the difference. But after 40 years of saving 10%, you will be sitting on $2.5 million that you might have blown on a bit more of what you already had. In this income range though, a key difference is that you have some major capital assets such as a house, a retirement fund, and a cottage. So why is saving important in this case? Aren't these assets a form of saving? Of course they are but they are not the liquid assets that form the basis of your financial flexibility. In other words, these are assets that bring financial stability instead of financial flexibility.

Selling the house is not a desirable option when your cash becomes tight. Neither is early withdrawal from a retirement account. These moves reduce your financial stability if they are done as a means to raise cash. You can always take on debt in this case, but is that what you really want? No, that just gets you more of what you don't want. Instead, saving gives you flexibility, liquidity, and practical desirable options.

No matter what your income level is, putting spending ahead of saving can cost you a large part of your mental contentment and your financial standard of living. In other words focusing on what you dislike about saving will distract you from what you actually like about it. Instead you can easily build a strong, secure financial base, simply by adopting the positive view of saving.

Fact # 6: Saving money works for everyone, regardless of income level.

The positive view of saving does not mean that you need to fret over every item you buy in order to save. If you are already disciplined about each daily purchase, then this path will add to your automatic savings and amplify your financial enjoyment. But if this kind of careful discipline is a major psychological change, then it may not be worthwhile. The path to saving should not be one of continuous mental torment. Instead, just stick with the automatic savings program and enjoy watching it work.

7 – Have A Cup of Coffee

Financial planners and budgeters make a lot of noise about take-out coffee. They say that you can save thousands every year if you stop buying coffee (or cigarettes or lunch). Although that is possible, you may not want to take it literally. The coffee example is only an illustration and it seems to work because it's so simple. But it causes a real problem. First, it doesn't work because people will seldom put $4 into a jar to actually save their coffee money. Second, it sets up a conflict between saving money and your basic desires. It says that you can only have one or the other, which makes saving money the sure loser.

In reality, saving money does not force you to give up your daily coffee or other small pleasures. That is just one option, if you are consistently able to make it work. If you are like most people though, without habits of strict discipline, then a budget is very unlikely to work because it demands a total change in your behavior: curbing your daily desires. Instead, by simply updating your view of saving money, you can get desire to work in your favor.

Let's look briefly at why saving money is harder than spending it. It boils down to a conflict between your immediate desires and your long-term desires. It's simply way easier to satisfy your desire for something right now. Just go ahead and buy it! At the same time though, you recognize that spending today prevents you from having more in the bank tomorrow. So how can you resolve this conflict? By creating a new way of looking at your long-term money.

Start by thinking of saved money as something you desire. Think of it as your pot of money, or as a big balance that you eagerly await in your monthly statement. And stop thinking about reducing your spending. In fact you can save money right up front from each paycheck, and then spend the rest on whatever you like. Coffee, shoes, dining, vacations, or anything else. If that is what you spend your money on, you can still enjoy the added freedom and power of saving money. Both desires are fulfilled. Watch your savings grow while you have another coffee. But there is one more crucial ingredient.

In order to feed this desire to have a pot of money, you should use a simple visual aid either on paper or on your computer. Make a little chart. Keep it very simple, like a growth chart that a parent makes for a child. Those simple tick marks on the door-frame at home kept track of a kid's height on various dates. The child kept watching those marks as he grew, and even though it was the easiest thing in the world to set up, he was always thrilled about it. Of course there was no doing involved, and no achievement, but it suited the child's mind very well. What about saving money for the adult or young adult mind?

A saving chart is just the same as a child's growth chart except that it keeps track of one of your main career achievements, your surplus earnings. This is what you work hard to build, so make sure to capture it and use it. Keep it handy to keep it front of mind. After all, this is your tactic to make sure that your long-term power stays as satisfying as your daily spending.

A simple chart works best. It only needs to show the amount of saving at a certain date, and you can add another date anytime you like. No matter if you add to it monthly or at each season, it will keep your savings growth fresh in mind and your desire will do the rest. Focus on your account balance and its growth. This is a major step in changing your mind for the better.

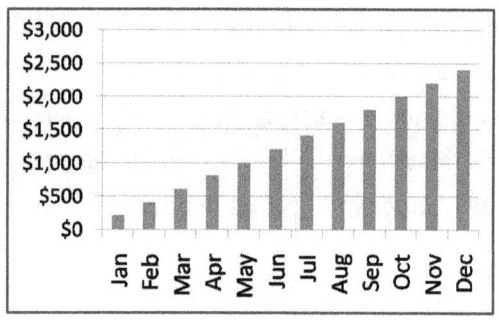

If you are new to making charts, start with a simple list on a page, like this...

MY SAVINGS

January $200
February $400
March $600
April $800
May $1000
June $1200
July $1400
August $1600
September $1800
October $2000
November $2200
December $2400

Make a list showing each month of the year. Beside each month, simply write down the total amount in your savings account. The benefit is that all of the information you need is in one place. You can see your progress with one glance. You cannot do this with your bank book because the numbers are spread out over many pages. A chart is even better than a list because once you draw it, you don't even need to read the numbers. You just look at the lines and see your savings grow.

Fact # 7 : a visual aid helps to make saving as rewarding as spending.

8 - Two Big Tips

So far we have avoided talking about daily tips for saving money. There are already dozens if not hundreds of books on that topic, so they won't be repeated here. Even so, the two most important tips deserve a mention to make sure that you don't miss the chance to benefit. Instead of worrying and scrimping on minor items, focus on the big items first. Housing and car, that's about as big as it gets. To do it right, you need to set it up right. And by making a couple of good up-front decisions, you can avoid thousands of dollars in unnecessary spending without even having to think about it again.

What can you do about car payments? Here's what you *could* do. Don't take a loan for a car. Instead, you could put the same amount in the bank every month for a year or two. If it's $500 a month, you will have $6,000 or $12,000 saved in the bank. Then you can go out and buy a good used car with cash, and you will have no monthly payments. Say that again to yourself… no monthly payments. Keep putting the $500 in the bank each month and watch your financial power grow. That's how to get ahead instead of falling behind.

If you decide to go ahead with this idea, don't buy a junker. A used car in poor condition will almost always be a financial drain for maintenance and emergency repairs. It will also tend to be unreliable and possibly an all-around hazard. To help you find a good car, read consumer reports, talk to someone who knows a lot about cars, and take the time to do a good deal of research. You can even talk to an insurance broker about which cars to avoid and which ones will cost you less to fix and insure.

What would have happened if you took the new car loan instead? For starters, you would have a new car that will shortly turn into a used car. And, by the way, this deteriorating used car will still cost you the same amount in ongoing monthly payments as when it was brand new. Not such a good deal.

Let's take a simple example using a middle-of-the-road Ford Fusion or similar new car at about

$25,000. Not the cheapest car, but not extravagant either. Add a couple of options and delivery charges (up to $1,600), and you are quickly near $30,000. And what about the taxes on a new car? If you borrow from the bank, you will be paying interest on the tax plus interest on the delivery! Likely for 4 years or more. On the plus side, you may be able to get regularly scheduled maintenance for no charge.

There are very few things more annoying or more useless than paying interest on taxes, so let's see how much extra that will be. Some US states impose no vehicle sales tax, but most will do so on new cars. Florida charges 6% new and used. Illinois ranges from 2 - 5%. Kentucky is at 6%. NY is at about 5%. In Canada, Alberta charges the least at 5%, while Quebec's 15% tops the list in major population regions.

Considering tax rates from across North America, the added cost can range from about $1,500 to $4,500. That raises your $30,000 loan to a high of $34,500. At a 5% annual interest rate over 4 years, it adds up to about $95 per month in interest. Most qualified financial advisors would likely tell you to avoid raising unnecessary monthly costs by that amount.

Here is a hypothetical example comparing some of the costs of a new car against a similar used car in good condition.

MONTHLY PAYMENT	USED paid with cash	NEW paid with a loan
Loan payment with interest	$0	$700
Interest on tax	$0	$95
Interest on delivery fee	$0	$35
Maintenance (estimated)	$100	$0
Total of monthly costs	$4,800	$39,840
ONE-TIME PAYMENT		
Down payment	$12,000	$0
Resale after 4 years	$2,000	$14,000
Total cost (capital, interest, maintenance)	$14,800	$25,840
Total cost per year	$3,700	$6,460
Total interest cost	$0	$3,795

If you buy a used car with your saved up cash, you can avoid some of the tax and all of the interest costs. Remember, this is not the total cost of car ownership. Total cost would also include fuel, insurance, and so on. This comparison illustrates the main differences between a new car bought with a loan, and a used car bought with cash.

In the above example, you could reduce your costs by $2,760 per year or $230 per month over 4 years. That's real money that you can save up to increase your financial power.

So it may seem obvious that you can make a real difference by saving up first, and avoiding a car loan. But now we're ready to get to the real point of this example. You will need to replace your car every few years. How will you buy the next one? With saved up money, of course.

Imagine that you bought the used car with saved up money. Now imagine that while you drive that car for 4 years, you also save up for the next car. How much could you save up? Let's say that you bank $800 per month, which is about the cost of a loan. At the end of 4 years, you would have

$38,400. Now you can go and buy a new car with no loan and no interest payments, if that's what suits you. Or better yet, you could buy another slightly used car, and invest the rest to earn more money. This cycle goes on for as long as you own a car. It's not just a 4 year loan, it's an ongoing loan for the rest of your driving life.

So let's reinforce the main point. Saving up to buy your first car means that you may be able to avoid paying loan interest *forever*. To do this, you simply keep saving as you go.

Conversely, if you take a loan, it almost certainly prevents you from being able to save for your next car. Taking a loan is almost like a trap that you may never escape.

Fact # 8 : a one-time car loan could turn into a *forever* loan.

If you buy a new car you will usually pay a far higher interest rate than your mortgage rate. Some people will say, yes, but a car loan only lasts a few years. Really? What will you do then? Stop driving? The fact is, if you felt the unavoidable urge to buy a new car once, you will probably feel it again when the loan is repaid. Then another new car comes along. Eventually you will have had a car loan all along, as long as a house mortgage. Interest payments were there all along, too.

To inform yourself better, find a suitable car on the manufacturer's website. Most car makers have a good price calculator. Then use the loan calculator on your bank's website. Play with various loan amounts and interest rates to get a good understanding of how they affect monthly payments. But also be sure to understand how much the total interest charges will be. That may be a big surprise for many people. Does $1,000 per year in interest payments sound like a good deal?

One important exception to the new car rule still stands out. For a daily commuter, a modest new car can sometimes be the right way to go. This will be a basic model with very few options, and it will be the long term car for the family, properly maintained for the long haul. It will not have leather seats or wide tires. If you must purchase it with a loan, the loan payments will be lower precisely because it's a basic model with cloth seats and narrow tires. Replacement tires will also be less costly. So will the inevitable replacement brakes, batteries, oil filters, insurance, and so on.

Finally, can you live near your work? Living close to work could make a whole list of vehicle costs a lot lower. Less driving means less fuel, less maintenance, and lower insurance, but the shorter daily drive to work also means that you'll have more time to do whatever you like to do. Spend less and live better?

It may not be possible for everyone, and some people prefer to live in a bigger house further from the main city in their region. But it also means that travel costs go up as housing prices fall. Does it balance out? Of course it depends on all of the details in your area, as long as you remember to include depreciation. A car used for long distance daily commuting will lose value faster than a short in-town commute. Could that cost be applied to a mortgage instead? Could a house within a city rise in value faster than a house in a suburb? It's worth your while to take a deep look before deciding.

—   —   —   —   —

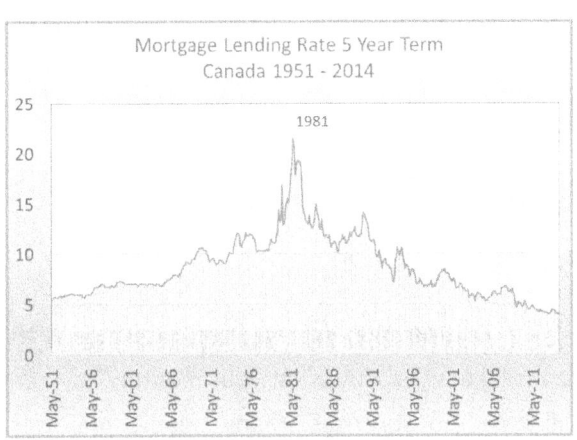

Source: derived from Statistics Canada Table 027-0015

Mortgage rates have been falling steadily since 1981. Household expenses could have fallen too. Instead, new houses keep getting bigger and pricier. Savings have fallen while personal debt has risen.

Is there a strategy for housing that leads to a stronger financial future without completely giving up on living in a house that you can enjoy?

Here is one approach you might consider, in 3 simple steps.

1 - Buy slightly less house than you can afford.
2 - Pay it down faster.
3 - Increase your savings & investment.

Then comes the oldest problem in the history of borrowing. Should you get a *fixed* or a *variable* interest rate?

On the plus side, a fixed rate means that you will know exactly what your monthly payments will be — no surprises. Many people prefer this option, thinking that it protects them in case interest rates go up. One flaw with this thinking is that if rates go up, you will likely still be forced to renew at that higher rate within a few years. And meanwhile you have been paying a higher rate because it was fixed.

The main problem is that a fixed rate costs more in interest charges than a variable rate mortgage. In other words, you will almost certainly pay more than the lowest possible rate right from the start. What should you do?

One approach is to ask a finance professor who has analyzed decades of information on mortgage payments. For example, York University professor Moshe Milevsky did just that and found that a variable rate is far more likely to reduce your overall cost of borrowing. By how much? It could amount to *tens of thousands of dollars,* so it's obviously very important. That also means it's worth the effort to read and understand these reports as well as discussing your own situation with a qualified financial advisor before deciding.

Can you predict interest rates better than the banks can? No. But perhaps the most surprising finding is that it would make no difference if you could. Knowing in advance that rates will rise at a particular time still would not help you to dodge the higher cost of a fixed rate. Read the reports carefully. You can find them here...

http://www.ifid.ca/newsletters.htm

(see the 2001 and 2004 reports on this page)

9 - An Unexpected Nudge

Full service stock brokers in some places are legally required to document the fact that they asked about a client's investment goals. This is the 'know your client' stuff. After all how can an advisor advise without knowing the client's goals? It seems that this question is also intended to make the client think a bit, exactly because many investors have no explicit goals. So the interesting part of this very ordinary multi-page questionnaire turns out to be a single point about retirement. This will come as no great surprise: it simply asks the client to state their expected retirement date.

The normal age of 65 should be comfortable for a lot of people after being immersed in that idea for most of their adult lives. But even after thinking about it for years, putting it on paper transforms the concept into a concrete commitment. That's not news to anyone who has been in any number of similar situations. Wedding vows are a very public display of commitment, making it more difficult to back out later. Journalists try to extract promises from campaigning politicians for the same reason: if it goes on record then it's more difficult to back out. You might not be able to imagine the force of it until you do it, especially if your goal is to retire early. So do it, write down your goal. Not because it's a magic bullet but because it just might help. It's a small concrete step, but it's also a huge psychological one.

10 - Finally Spending What You Save

What about spending? Is it always bad? It depends on what kinds of things you spend your money on. One of the best purchases is something that produces more money and more financial freedom. That could be an investment or a business or an education (fill in the blank here with more of your own good ideas). This kind of spending can end up adding to your saving and increasing your financial power. There is always some risk that these ventures don't pan out, but they are not a throwaway.

On the other hand, one of the worst purchases is something that costs money you don't have, and then deteriorates. As we already said, the best example is a new car. There is nothing wrong with buying a new car at a price level that matches your income. If you can't buy one with saved up cash though, you will spend on interest payments for years while the car wears out. It will become worthless after draining your finances.

There is little joy in having a car that only felt new for a year before it got scratched, dented, and worn. And even that is not the whole story. What happens when the car is finally sold or scrapped? Of course the cycle starts all over again with then next car and its interest payments. Over a lifetime, the interest payments have added up to several cars that you never had a chance to own. Better to save for the first one, or at least to be aware of what's at stake before making the decision to spend.

So there turns out to be two kinds of spending. Spending your income, and spending your main savings. Once you put away the first 10% of your income, you can practically spend the rest on whatever you like. If that is coffee, cars, vacations then that's just fine. You are already building your financial base with your savings.

But there must be another point to all that saving in addition to the peace of mind and flexibility that it has brought. Shouldn't it eventually be spent on something big? Of course it should. And the final point is that spending your savings is best suited to productive items, real emergencies, or living in retirement.

Emergencies and retirement are fairly straightforward. If you unexpectedly lose your job, savings can be used to fill the income gap. You already built up your savings once, so you know how to rebuild it after finding another job. Retirement spending isn't an urgent issue so put aside thinking about that as you get well practiced at enjoying your savings. Meanwhile, you can take your time and find a retirement planner who makes sense to you.

Finally, productive spending items are those that can create more savings and power for you, like getting an education or starting a business. Not education like golf lessons, but something that can increase your job earnings and generate more savings. And not a risky fantasy business that you don't know anything about, but rather something that you know well enough to understand the real game.

Maximize the benefit and minimize the risk. The real point behind the productive kind of spending is that it adds to your personal safety net and lets you enjoy every day without worry. Is that kind of fun worth saving up for? You decide.

If you enjoyed this book, please consider writing a review on Amazon.com or your favorite bookseller's website.

Please follow me on Twitter @joe_atikian
or visit www.atikian.com